Building Brand Awareness with Specialty Advertising and Promotional Items

A Step by Step Guide

By Meir Liraz

(Including 10 Special Bonuses)

Published by Liraz Publishing

www.BizMove.com

Copyright © Liraz Publishing. All rights reserved.

ISBN: 9781696396059

Table of Contents

1. Introduction — 5
2. Why Specialty Advertising Works — 7
3. Elements of a Promotion — 12
4. Typical Promotion Applications — 17

Supplement:

5. How to Create a Marketing Plan — 23

Appendix: Special Free Bonuses — 42

MEIR LIRAZ

1. Introduction

For years business owners have been putting their names and logos on such things as calendars, notepads, ball-point pens and keytags and giving them to customers and prospects. Not intended simply as an act of business generosity, this is advertising specialty advertising to be exact. The problem is that many small business owners don't know the fine points of this form of advertising and don't maximize the advantages it offers. This guide explains why specialty advertising works and provides illustrations of how small business firms have applied this targeted medium to specific promotional objectives achieving some remarkable results.

An industrial film studio once ran an ad headlined: It's more important to reach the people who count than to count the people you reach. That is a handy maxim for business owners to keep in mind when they plan their advertising, because money spent on reaching the people who don't count-non-prospects-is money wasted.

This fact is acknowledged by your life insurance agent who gives you a calendar each year or by your bank that gives you a ball-point pen with the bank name on it. As a policyholder and as a depositor, you count with these businesses, and they give you these promotional items-properly called advertising specialties-to let you know it.

The fact these items are given away shouldn't be misinterpreted as purely an act of business charity. There is a reason for presenting specialty advertising gifts. When used properly, specialty advertising can be one of the most effective means of promoting a small business. The trick is to use it properly. But first business owners must understand what it is and what it can and cannot do for their companies.

2. Why Specialty Advertising Works

Advertising specialties are defined as useful articles of merchandise that are imprinted with an advertisement and are given to customers and potential customers without any strings attached. Unlike premiums, they are not earned or awarded in exchange for a purchase. Sometimes the ad on these specialties is no more than the name or logo of the sponsor. Everyday one comes across cigarette lighters, ashtrays, paperweights, ball-point pens and T-shirts that meet this description. These are just a few of the estimated 15,000 different types of merchandising items that are used in the medium called specialty advertising.

All advertising media offer users specific advantages-and all media have their limitations. You must be familiar with the strengths and weaknesses of the various media in order to make the right choices for your business.

Let's look at some of the advantages offered by specialty advertising.

Unlike newspapers and television, which are mass media, specialty advertising is one of the targeted media. Newspapers and television are fine when you want to deliver your message to the most people you can possibly reach. But in this mass audience are many people who are not interested in what you have to sell. Consequently, you must also look for promotional efficiency. This is provided by the targeted media-direct mail, trade press and specialty advertising-because they can deliver your message only to prospects, thereby saving you the expense of buying non-productive circulation.

Notice that specialty advertising products are defined as useful articles of merchandise. Because they are useful, at least to varying degrees, they are kept and used by recipients. Each time the items are referred to, the advertiser's name and message get exposure. The recipient doesn't always consciously note the ad, of course, but the message is entered into the individual's memory and can be recalled at the appropriate time.

Advertising recall is important, but so often advertisers don't achieve this sought-after benefit from the media they use. What good does it do when the TV viewer chuckles over a clever commercial but can't remember the name of the sponsor?

When it comes to ad budgets, small businesses obviously cannot compete with corporate giants. Budget limitations severely restrict the small entrepreneur's use of some of the costlier mass media. Fortunately, specialty advertising comes in a lot of price ranges. There are, remember, 15,000 different types of specialties, some costing several dollars and some only a few cents apiece. So there are specialties available to any advertiser, regardless of how small the budget.

How consumers react to your advertising is important. If they are offended or indifferent to it, you have not gained from your promotional investment. Specialty advertising, however, carries with it an ingratiation factor. People like to get something for nothing, regardless of how inexpensive the item may be. They tend to look favorably on companies giving them free specialties. There is statistical evidence that people prefer to patronize businesses giving specialties as opposed to those that do not, all things being equal.

Another unique attribute of specialty advertising is that it permits advertisers to personalize the message. Suppose out of all your customers and prospects there are a hundred or so key ones you want to concentrate on. Because you probably can identify them by name, you can give added value to the advertising item you send them by imprinting their name on it. The favorable reaction to this kind of message enhancement can never be overstated.

As you can see, there are several advantages offered by specialty advertising, some of which cannot be found in other media. Specialties also have some limitations. One has to do with the amount of copy space available. On a ball-point pen, for example, there usually isn't enough space to imprint more than the advertiser's name and address. To overcome this deficiency, advertisers often distribute a printed companion piece with the specialty, and this flyer or brochure contains the reasons to purchase.

Another liability is the comparatively long production and delivery time sometimes required to implement a specialty advertising promotion. Even stock items ordered right out of a manufacturer's catalog sometimes take four to eight weeks for delivery. Consequently, the business owner who plans to hold a clearance sale the following week may find his or her purpose better served by using newspaper ads and TV or radio spots.

Another drawback worth mentioning is the difficulty one finds in measuring the results of many specialty promotions. Of course, this is a problem with other media, too. Unless a method of evaluation is built into the specialty promotion, the business owner may have no evidence the promotion is doing him or her any good. Indeed, some types of promotions offer no practical means of measuring their effectiveness. This doesn't mean the promotion shouldn't be undertaken. A simple promotion to achieve goodwill for the business owner may do just that, but it is difficult to weigh that goodwill and translate it into sales.

3. Elements of a Promotion

You should not confuse a planned promotion with a simple distribution of specialties. Promotions require considerable forethought and work and, consequently, they are likely to be much more productive. Promotions are composed of a number of elements:

Establishing objectives

Defining target audiences

Adopting a distribution method

Developing a theme and copy

Selecting the appropriate specialties

Implementing the promotion

Evaluating the results

Objectives. No one advertises without a reason and an expectation of accomplishment. However, sometimes the reasons and the expectations are not clearly understood and stated. Unless you set forth at the beginning realistic objectives, consistent with your budget, you become a traveler embarking on a trip without any conception of how or where you're going.

Target audiences. These are the prospects for your business. Sometimes they are qualified on the basis of probable use of your products or services: heavy users and light users. Greater promotional weight may then be applied to the heavy users' group that will produce more revenue for your business. You may recall the adage that 80 percent of a firm's business comes from 20 percent of its customers.

Distribution method. Specialties are distributed to the targeted prospects in a number of ways: over the counter in the advertiser's place of business; by a second party whose business is related in some way to the advertiser or its customers; by direct mail solicitation; and by sales people calling on prospects.

Proper attention to distribution is essential, because the promotion will fail if the specialties don't reach the right people.

Theme and copy. The theme is what gives a promotion an identity, ties it together and makes it memorable. The copy that appears on the specialties and the accompanying product or service literature should relate to that theme. If you are mounting a full-fledged campaign involving other media, be sure you coordinate the specialties with the over-all campaign theme.

Selection of specialties. This is a key element that should not be slighted. It involves much more than examining a couple of catalogs and choosing a specialty that catches your eye.

In making your selection, you must first, of course, consider your budget. Suppose you've allocated $1,000 to purchase specialties and you have in mind a target audience of 1,000 persons. This means your choice is limited to specialties costing no more than $1 apiece. If you think a higher-ticket item will be more effective, you can reduce your intended target audience to, say, 250 persons, thus allowing for a $4 item. Another alternative is to increase your budget. You can also make a stratified distribution, whereby the higher priced specialties are directed to the best prospects and the lower-priced items are distributed to lesser prospects.

The next thing to be examined is the desired audience reaction. If you are simply trying to get noticed, an attention-getter is required. This can be anything from a balloon or novelty item like the giant Styrofoam We're Number One fingers. On the other hand, if you want to be remembered over a period of time, choose a specialty that is more useful and practical and, hence, more likely to be retained by the recipients.

Your distribution method must be considered, too, when you select specialties. For example, if you intend to mail the specialties to your target audience, you should either consider the weight and size of the articles or add to your postage budget.

Whenever possible, the specialties should be related in some way to your product or service, to your target audience, or to your promotion theme. This is why optometrists often use packets of eyeglass lens tissues to promote their practices and why auto dealers give keytags to prospective car buyers. The association between the specialty and the advertiser or the item and the audience usage has the effect of triggering audience recall.

Implementation. This is the point where the promotion strategy is executed. It involves not only distributing the specialties to the target audience but also securing whatever information and cooperation is needed to make the promotion work. Examples of implementation will be described in the next section covering typical promotion objectives.

Evaluation. This is something that is often ignored because it is either impractical in relation to the promotional investment or because the response is difficult to measure. Yet whenever possible, business owners should try to get a reading on the promotional efficiency of all media they use because it helps them determine whether the promotion should be repeated, revised or discontinued and whether or not the budget is sufficient. Promotions employing a direct mail solicitation, for example, are easy to measure. All you need to do is make a split-run mailing in which half the audience gets the specialty and product literature and the other half gets only the literature. Then you compare the response rates between the two audience segments.

4. Typical Promotion Applications

There are hundreds of applications for specialty advertising. These are some of the most frequent uses by small businesses:

Celebrating grand openings or special events

Building store traffic

Developing or qualifying business leads

Promoting image and maintaining customer goodwill

Introducing new products and services

Opening doors for salespeople

Grand openings and special events. Whether a business is brand new in town or has been around awhile, it needs to make prospects aware of its existence. One of the best ways is to bring prospects to the establishment so they can see for themselves what the firm's . capabilities are.

Example: Management of a welding and metal fabricator wanted a large turnout at its open house and wished to assure that guests saw every phase of production. The invitation promised each guest an unidentified gift for attending. In addition, prizes were to be awarded at random. Since it was impossible to give each guest an escorted tour, prize stations were set up in each work area. Guests were given their gift, a pewter letter opener embossed with the advertiser's logo, and an itinerary showing the prize stations. At each station was an RFD-type mailbox containing an envelope that could be slit with the letter opener. The message inside indicated if guests had won a prize or should try their luck at the next station. Of the 797 persons invited, 575 attended and toured the entire facility.

Store traffic. Specialty advertising can help develop patronage. All it takes is a little imagination.

Example: Owners of a restaurant specializing in French cuisine and fine wines believed the best way to increase their patronage was to go after the affluent market. They targeted 500 upper income families new to the area and sent them a linen wall calendar on which was imprinted the recipe of the restaurant's famous shrimp Creole. Recipients were told they could get a free cocktail for each member of their party with purchased meals if they presented the hanger string of the calendar. Fifty-two percent of the targeted households took advantage of the free cocktail offer, and many respondents became regular customers.

Developing leads. Who is really in the market for your product or service? They need to be identified and made aware of what you have to offer.

Example: A personnel placement agency ran an ad in a business journal announcing The Grant Texas Type-off in which secretaries and other typists could compete for a prize trip to Acapulco. Specialties were chosen to conform to the promotion's western theme. Agency employees wore T-shirts imprinted with the Wanted-poster theme of the Type-off, and name badges resembling sheriff's stars were issued to the fast-typing finalists, judges and members of the press. Media reporters were also issued theme-imprinted tote bags and T-shirts. The competition produced good media coverage and 400 entrants. The sponsoring agency obtained 100 new placement candidates and 50 new companies for its client list.

Promoting image and goodwill. Reliability, quality products, fair prices, fast service; concern for customers are typical images businesses like to portray. Specialties can help, too.

Example: A plumbing supply company mailed a survey questionnaire to plumbing contractors. Copy on an accompanying cartoon explained the firm valued the recipients' business and wanted their opinion of the company's performance, because We want to be sure to measure up. To elicit a response, the mailer contained a logo-imprinted tape measure, chosen because of its association with the theme- Measure Up. The mailing generated a 35 percent return, enabling the company to correct service deficiencies.

Introducing new products and services. When you're offering prospects something they haven't seen before from you (or perhaps from anyone else), you've got to tell them about it.

Example: a purchaser of a materials-handling equipment distributorship quickly sought to divorce itself from the previous owner's reputation for poor service. The new owner mailed to 425 prospects a card introducing a cartoon character, Super Hustler, who was described as being faster than a speeding piston, more powerful than a C-500, and able to cut overhead in a single call. The new service policy was amplified in a second mailing that guaranteed a repair man on the scene within three hours of a call.

Imprinted on the enclosed specialty, a shoulder phone rest, was the number to call for service. The final mailing promised another specialty, a coffee mug, for those who returned a reply card. Approximately 50 percent of the recipients requested a coffee mug, which was delivered by a salesperson. The new service policy and its imaginative proclamation helped increase the distributor's service business 27 percent.

Opening doors for salespeople. Few salespeople are so presumptuous as to think prospects are waiting to receive them with a brass band. More often, the prospect is "in conference," "out of town," "can't be disturbed," or is otherwise unavailable to the salesperson. And when direct mail is used, often there is a secretary who is screening the mail. What is needed is a door opener.

Example: Telephone solicitation was being used by a sales training organization to arrange appointments for its salespeople. Because it was securing only four appointments for every ten calls, the company decided to try something else. The firm's specialty advertising counselor recommended designing a custom specialty-an 11 ounce bar of chocolate molded into the shape of a giant baby pacifier. The item tied in nicely to the accompanying copy: Instead of trying to pacify salesmen whose sales are declining, show them how to improve. Attractively gift-wrapped, the pacifier was delivered to the target audience without the sender's name on the box so the recipient would have to open the package to find out who sent it. The idea worked. It achieved for the sales trainer a 90 percent appointment rate, and these calls produced an 80 percent closing rate.

Success stories like these do not come about by accident. These advertisers wanted results and looked for someone who could deliver them.

5. How to Create a Marketing Plan

The marketing plan is a problem-solving document. Skilled problem solvers recognize that a big problem is usually the combination of several smaller problems. The best approach is to solve each of the smaller problems first, thereby dividing the big problem into manageable pieces. Your marketing plan should take the same approach. It should be a guide on which to base decisions and should ensure that everyone in your organization is working together to achieve the same goals. A good marketing plan can prevent your organization from reacting to problems in a piecemeal manner and even help in anticipating problems.

Before your marketing plan can be developed, research must give you the basic guidelines: for whom you are designing your product or service (market segmentation), and exactly what that product or service should mean to those in the marketplace (market positioning). Below are some guidelines to help you develop a marketing plan to support the strategy you have selected for your organization.

Market Segmentation

Your marketing plan should recognize the various segments of the market for your product or service and indicate how to adjust your product to reach those distinct markets. Instead of marketing a product in one way to everyone, you must recognize that some segments are not only different, but better than others for your product. This approach can be helpful in penetrating markets that would be too broad and undefined without segmentation. No matter what you are making or selling, take the total market and divide it up like a pie chart. The divisions can be based on various criteria such as those listed below.

Demographics

This is the study of the distribution, density and vital statistics of a population, and includes such characteristics as

Sex.

Age.

Education.

Geographic location.

Home ownership versus rental.

Marital status.

Size of family unit.

Total income of family unit.

Ethnic or religious background.

Job classification blue collar versus salaried or professional.

Psychographics

This is the study of how the human characteristics of consumers may have a bearing on their response to products, packaging, advertising and public relations efforts. Behavior may be measured as it involves an interplay among these broad sets of variables:

Predisposition - What is there about a person's past culture, heredity or upbringing that may influence his or her ability to consider purchasing one new product or service versus another?

Influences - What are the roles of social forces such as education, peer pressure or group acceptance in dictating a person's consumption patterns?

Product Attributes - What the product is or can be made to represent in the minds of consumers has a significant bearing on whether certain segments will accept the concept. These attributes may be suggested by the marketer or perceived by the customer. Some typical ways of describing a product include:

Price/value perception - Is the item worth the price being asked?

Taste - Does it have the right amount of sweetness or lightness?

Texture - Does it have the accepted consistency or feel?

Quality - What can be said about the quality of the ingredients or lack of artificial ingredients?

Benefits - How does the consumer feel after using the product?

Trust - Can the consumer rely on this particular brand? What about the reputation of the manufacturer in standing behind the product?

Life-Style

Statements consumers make about themselves

through conspicuous consumption can be put to good use by research people who read the signals correctly. By studying behavioral variables, such as a person's use of time, services and products, researchers can identify some common factors that can predict future behavior.

Market Positioning

You must realize that your product or service cannot be all things to all people. Very few items on the market today have universal appeal. Even when dealing in basic commodities like table salt or aspirin, marketing people have gone to all sorts of extremes to create brand awareness and product differentiation. If your product or service is properly positioned, prospective purchasers or users should immediately recognize its unique benefits or advantages and be better able to assess it in comparison to your competition's offering. Positioning is how you give your product or service brand identification.

Positioning involves analyzing each market segment as defined by your research activities and developing a distinct position for each segment. Ask yourself how you want to appear to that segment, or what you must do for that segment to ensure that it buys your product or service. This will dictate different media and advertising appeals for each segment. For example, you may sell the same product in a range of packages or sizes, or make cosmetic changes in the product, producing private labels or selecting separate distribution channels to reach the various segments. Beer, for example, is sold on tap and in seven-ounce bottles, twelve-ounce cans and bottles, six-packs, twelve-packs, cases, and quart bottles and kegs of several sizes. The beer is the same but each package size may appeal to a separate market segment and have to be sold with a totally different appeal and through different retail outlets.

Remember that your marketing position can, and should, change to meet the current conditions of the market for your product. The ability of your company to adjust will be enhanced greatly by an up-to-date knowledge of the marketplace gained through continual monitoring. By having good data about your customers, the segments they fit into and the buying motives of those segments, you can select the position that makes the most sense.

While there are many possible marketing positions,

most would fit into one of the following categories:

Positioning on specific product features - A very common approach, especially for industrial products. If your product or service has some unique features that have obvious value this may be the way to go.

Positioning on benefits - Strongly related to positioning on product features. Generally, this is more effective because you can talk to your customers about what your product or service can do for them. The features may be nice, but unless customers can be made to understand why the product will benefit them, you may not get the sale.

Positioning for a specific use - Related to benefit positioning. Consider Campbell's positioning of soups for cooking. An interesting extension is mood positioning: "Have a Coke and a smile." This works best when you can teach your customers how to use your product or when you use a promotional medium that allows a demonstration.

Positioning for user category - A few examples: "You've Come a Long Way Baby," "The Pepsi Generation" and "Breakfast of Champions." Be sure you show your product being used by models with whom your customers can identify.

Positioning against another product or a competing business - A strategy that ranges from implicit to explicit comparison. Implicit comparisons can be quite pointed; for example, Avis never mentions Hertz, but the message is clear. Explicit comparisons can take two major forms. The first form makes a comparison with a direct competitor and is aimed at attracting customers from the compared brand, which is usually the category leader. The second type does not attempt to attract the customers of the compared product, but rather uses the comparison as a reference point. Consider, for example, the positioning of the Volkswagen Dasher, which picks up speed faster than a Mercedes and has a bigger trunk than a Rolls Royce. This usually works to the advantage of the smaller business if you can capitalize on the tradition of cheering for the underdog. You can gain stature by comparing yourself to a larger competitor just as long as your customers remain convinced that you are trying harder.

Product class disassociation - A less common type of positioning. It is particularly effective when used to introduce a new product that differs from traditional products. Lead-free gasoline and tubeless tires were new product classes positioned against older products. Space-age technology may help you here. People have become accustomed to change and new products and are more willing to experiment than was true ten years ago. Even so, some people are more adventuresome and trusting than others and more apt to try a revolutionary product. The trick is to find out who are the potential brand switchers or experimenters and find out what it would take to get them to try your product. The obvious disadvantage of dealing with those who try new products is that they may move on to another brand just as easily. Brand loyalty is great as long as it is to your brand.

Hybrid bases - Incorporates elements from several types of positioning. Given the variety of possible bases for positioning, small business owners should consider the possibility of a hybrid approach. This is particularly true in smaller towns where there aren't enough customers in any segment to justify the expense of separate marketing approaches.

MEIR LIRAZ

MARKETING PLAN WORKSHEET

This is the marketing plan of _____

I. MARKET ANALYSIS

A. Target Market - Who are the customers?

1. We will be selling primarily to (check all that apply):

Percent of Business

a. Private sector _____

b. Wholesalers _____

c. Retailers _____

d. Government _____

e. Other _____

2. We will be targeting customers by:

a. Product line/services. We will target specific lines _____

b. Geographic area? Which areas? _____

c. Sales? We will target sales of _____

d. Industry? Our target industry is
_____

e. Other? _____

3. How much will our selected market spend on our type of product or service this coming year?

_____

B. Competition

1. Who are our competitors?

Name _____

Address _____

Years in Business _____

Market Share _____

Price/Strategy _____

Product/Service _____

Features _____

Name _____

Address _____

Years in Business _____

Market Share _____

Price/Strategy _____

Product/Service _____

Features _____

2. How competitive is the market?

High _____

Medium _____

Low _____

3. List below your strengths and weaknesses compared to your competition (consider such areas as location, size of resources, reputation, services, personnel, etc.):

Strengths

1_____

2_____

3_____

4_____

Weaknesses

1_____

2_____

3_____

4_____

C. Environment

1. The following are some important economic factors that will affect our product or service (such as country growth, industry health, economic trends, taxes, rising energy prices, etc.):

_____

_____

_____

2. The following are some important legal factors that will affect our market:

_____

_____

_____

3. The following are some important government factors:

_____

_____

_____

4. The following are other environmental factors that will affect our market, but over which we have no control:

_____

_____

_____

II. PRODUCT OR SERVICE ANALYSIS

A. Description

1. Describe here what the product/service is and what it does:

_____

_____

_____

B. Comparison

1. What advantages does our product/service have over those of the competition (consider such things

as unique features, patents, expertise, special training, etc.)?

_____

_____

_____

2. What disadvantages does it have?

_____

_____

_____

C. Some Considerations

1. Where will you get your materials and supplies?

_____

2. List other considerations:

_____

_____

_____

III. MARKETING STRATEGIES - MARKET MIX

A. Image

1. First, what kind of image do we want to have (such as cheap but good, or exclusiveness, or customer-oriented or highest quality, or convenience, or speed, or ...)?

_____

B. Features

1. List the features we will emphasize:

a. _____

b. _____

c. _____

C. Pricing

1. We will be using the following pricing strategy:

a. Markup on cost _____ What % Markup? _____

b. Suggested price _____

c. Competitive _____

d. Below competition _____

e. Premium price ____

f. Other ____

2. Are our prices in line with our image?

YES ___ NO ___

3. Do our prices cover costs and leave a margin of profit?

YES ___ NO ___

D. Customer Services

1. List the customer services we provide:

a. _____

b. _____

c. _____

2. These are our sales/credit terms:

a. _____

b. _____

c. _____

3. The competition offers the following services:

a. _____

b. _____

c. _____

E. Advertising/Promotion

1. These are the things we wish to say about the business:

_____

_____

_____

2. We will use the following advertising/promotion sources:

1. Television _____

2. Radio _____

3. Online: Google (AdWords) / Facebook

4. Direct mail _____

5. Personal contacts _____

6. Trade associations _____

7. Newspaper _____

8. Magazines _____

9. Yellow Pages _____

10. Billboard _____

11. Other _____

3. The following are the reasons why we consider the media we have chosen to be the most effective:

_____

_____

Appendix: Special Free Bonuses

You can access your free bonuses here:

https://www.bizmove.com/bizgifts.htm

Here's what you get:

#1 How to Be a Good Manager and Leader; 120 Tips to improve your Leadership Skills (Leadership Video Guide).

Learn how to improve your leadership skills and become a better manager and leader. Here's how to be the boss people want to give 200 percent for. In this video you'll discover 120 powerful tips and strategies to motivate and inspire your people to bring out the best in them.

#2 Small Business Management: Essential Ingredients for Success (eBook Guide)

Discover scores of business management tricks, secrets and shortcuts. This Ebook guide does far more than impart knowledge - it inspires action.

#3 How to Manage Yourself for Success; 90 Tips to Better Manage Yourself and Your Time (Self Management Video Guide)

You are responsible for everything that happens in your life. Learn to accept total responsibility for yourself. If you don't manage yourself, then you are letting others have control of your life. In this video you'll discover 90 powerful tips and strategies to better manage yourself for success.

#4 80 Best Inspirational Quotes for Success (Motivational Video Guide)

For this video we scanned thousands of motivational and inspirational quotes to bring you this collection of the best 80 motivational quotes for success in life.

#5 Top 10 Habits to Adopt From Highly Successful People (Self Growth Video Guide)

In this video you'll discover the top 10 habits of highly successful people that you can adopt and achieve success in your life.

#6 Personal Branding: How to Make a Killer First Impression (Self Promotion Video Guide)

This video deals with personal branding. While promoting your personal brand, you'll discover in this video the ten most effective things you can do to make the best first impression possible.

#7 How to Advance Your Career 10 Times Faster (Career Advancement Video Guide)

The most important thing to remember about your

career today is that you need to be responsible for your own future. In this video you'll discover 10 powerful strategies to advance your career faster.

#8 How to Get Success in Life; 10 Strategies to Attract the Life You Want (Self Actualization Video Guide)

To have more, we must be more of who we are. The secret is in the doing; none of it matters until we do something about it. In this video you'll discover 10 powerful strategies to attract the life you want.

#9 A Comprehensive Package of Business Tools

Here's a collection featuring dozens of business related templates, worksheets, forms, and plans; covering finance, starting a business, marketing, business planning, sales, and general management.

#10 People Management Skills: How to Deal with Difficult Employees (Managing People Video Guide)

Problem behavior on the part of employees can erupt for a variety of reasons. In this video you'll discover the top ten ideas for dealing with difficult employees.

BUILDING BRAND AWARENESS

* * * *

www.ingramcontent.com/pod-product-compliance
Lightning Source LLC
Chambersburg PA
CBHW070840220526
45466CB00002B/838